LIVI
LOVI RIEF

Sharon Rose

Photographs
by
Faith White

ARTHUR H. STOCKWELL LTD
Torrs Park Ilfracombe Devon
Established 1898
www.ahstockwell.co.uk

British Library Cataloguing-in-Publication Data.
A catalogue record for this book is available from the British Library.

ISBN 978-0-7223-4069-1
Printed in Great Britain by
Arthur H. Stockwell Ltd
Torrs Park Ilfracombe
Devon

Dedication

This book is dedicated to my mum, who lost her son, and my sister, Helen, who lost her brother, Adrian William Bailey, 8 June 1969 to 5 March 2009.

You are a star and we miss you.

I'm not as brave as Adrian, nowhere near. He has escaped the silence and cut off from his broken heart. He has stopped the suffocation of loneliness. On 25 February 2009 my brother hanged himself to 'Ten Storey Love Song' by Stone Roses . Could he call for help? No, he had no credit. Should he drink or eat? Drink is preferred as it numbs the mind and keeps the matter in hand clearly focused. He had spent a long time planning and building his own gallows. He made sure we wouldn't find out until after my birthday (28 February). When he didn't show for my birthday celebration we knew deep in our hearts something was not quite right.

On 5 March the police broke through the barricade and there he was, gone from this world. That day, 5 March, became the start of another era.

How could you take your life when I had fought so hard to keep mine? Why? Why? Initially we were on automatic pilot, intent on getting every detail of the funeral right – and we planned this around your life. The Beatles were chosen to guide you into your funeral and you, by choice, sung yourself out. If you had been able to look around, you'd have seen the enormity of sadness in the eyes of those you loved the most in the world.

My mum's heart is broken, my sister's the same. And there is nothing I can do to help them because mine is splintered too.

So we watched over and over again videos of Adrian at his happiest, as lead singer and lead guitarist with his group The Diversions. He had such a natural talent and we were so proud of him. I used to manage his group and we managed to get a spot on a daytime television programme, *Daytime Live*, with Sarah Kennedy hosting the show. The Diversions were all about sixteen years old at the time, and they played out the show with 'Hard Day's Night'. Lulu and Sandy Shaw were the other guests, and my mum and ex-husband were there too. We were still watching the video when the priest came round to get a picture of Adrian before the funeral.

We showed him the videos of you singing; we showed him you as we want to remember you.

Suddenly, while we were watching you, the telly just switched itself off. We all looked at one another and the priest broke the silence. He said, "Sometimes these things happen." What a surreal moment that was!

I cried when we went to empty Adrian's flat. There

was a feeling of unreality, as though we had stepped into a scene from a horror movie. My sister, Helen, my stepbrothers, my stepfather, Mike, and my son, Alistair, were with me. I don't know whether I should have taken Alistair, but I needed his shoulder to lean on. That day he went from boy to man.

We walked aimlessly around the flat, looking for hidden clues to help us understand why he didn't ask us to help. Yes, he lived on his own, but the flat was clean and tidy; there were no visible clues to his poverty or sadness, only the homemade gallows and the carefully planned barricade at the door. And where he had taken his life there were marks in the carpet where they had laid him down.

This is the only time I cried. I was frantically clinging to Helen's renewed faith in the Catholic religion. She had brought candles, prayers and holy water. I begged her to sprinkle some holy water on the place where he died, and her prayers helped me know he had been forgiven for taking his life. I didn't feel his presence in the flat.

He has gone to – I hope with all my heart – a place of peace, where food is free, where love is genuine and unconditional, where smiling faces are the only rule and guitars play. He has found peace first, while we are still searching the highs and lows of life.

I had brushed with death myself and, although not ready to join Adrian, I want to believe there is something for us after death.

I am not at liberty to speculate.

I knew another thing: I was going to go through this experience without a partner's shoulder to cry on, but being single and dealing with cancer had strengthened me. My rejection at Christmas, only two months before Adrian's death, had also given me extra durability to cope with life events alone. I just needed my mum and my sister. The bond between us demonstrated the truth behind the saying 'Blood is thicker than water'. We clung to each other.

Life is so fragile.

WHY NO TEARS? WHAT, NO CRY?

What, no cry, no cry, no cry?
My brother's gone we don't know why.
I cannot feel; my soul is lost;
I cannot face reality at any cost.
I cannot begin to feel
Or allow thoughts of him to enter my head.
Once memories of childhood stories seep into my mind,
Then all those years in tears will be shed.
But no cry – why, oh why, no cry?
Just anger ahead.

Time goes by. Where are you? We can't reach you.
We can't see you, we can't touch you.
Why are you walking away from me?
I can't see the smile on your face.
I search the world to find you again.
My search is fruitless –
There is no trace.

Only in my heart there lies a picture of you.
A birthday will appear and we can only remember the past –
Birthday years when the jigsaw of family life was complete.
We laughed and we cheered, rich with family love.
Bring on my tears!
Why no tears? Why no cry?

I didn't even say goodbye.

18 March 2009, 1.08 a.m.

Here I am again ALONE in the middle of the night, dreading the next day, the final goodbye, the funeral. I have seen no one all day except Helen very briefly to look at the flowers on the coffin – a guitar-shaped flower arrangement.

I am lying here, teeth clenched with anger at life events. My ears are bursting with the most aggravating noise in the world: SILENCE.

The Funeral

What is significant about this funeral is that there shouldn't have been one. I felt as though I had one of the lead roles in a feature film and was shaking hands with all the cast of Adrian's life – so many friends and people who thought a lot of him, admired his music and respected his great talent. This is the irony: you may be alone all your life, but the day you won't be alone is your funeral.

The moral of the story is to always say "Hello" and "How are you?" to one friend a day.

We put on Adrian's death certificate 'Musician'. Why didn't we call him a musician when he was alive, instead of unemployed? We met his friends and understood him more, but it was too late. I had thought myself open to all lessons to be learnt.

Ms Rose, you think you are a totally non-judgemental person. Ha ha, think again! You have learnt a valuable lesson. Start looking closer to home,

Sharon, and appreciate your own daughter's pastime. Fiona enjoys pole dancing, and it takes a lot of strength to swing on those poles and a lot of guts to face the stereotypical prejudices and gazes of disgust when people find out what you do. I have to have strength too, as I sometimes feel as if I am judged too – but whatever, Fiona, I will always love you.

That's exactly what my mum did: she cast off the comments about the unemployed, the poverty, the life choice Adrian made, and she continued to support him and help him. She can rest assured that as a mum she fulfilled her role and did all she could to prevent her son's tragic death. She could have done no more.

Adrian's death leaves us all with lessons to be learnt. We maybe need to question our actions sometimes, such as when we have silly, pointless rows with family and fall out and spend many days not speaking. I have known this amongst families; and if we look closer, most of us can find examples amongst our very own loved ones.

On 19 March we went as a family to look at the flowers and walk. Is it just us? We hadn't an idea about what happens to our loved ones after a cremation. We were given the option of scattering the ashes in the rose garden, but there is no rose garden. Ashes mingle together on patches of green grass. I was horrified and I ran to the office to make sure they kept Adrian's ashes. Mum chose his final destination and we were to have a private service to scatter them.

When I'm gone I want a place for me to rest and for my children to come and say hello every now and again so that I can still be, in name only, a part of this world.

This does lead me to a situation I found myself in a few months down the line when I discovered that my partner, Chris, still had his wife's ashes in a cupboard.

What! And you say you have let go!

I was insistent that I was no way going to go to Daisy Lane with his wife still there. I would not be part of a threesome, dead or alive. I was also thinking about the girls: all they had was a cupboard to go to instead of a respectful place of rest for their mum.

This was the weirdest time ever. How we stayed together I don't know. I really felt as though I was in a film as the vile mistress who is going out with the husband before the wife is even in her grave.

We were very distant and totally emotionally up in the air. Chris told me to think about our own wedding. He was clinging desperately, afraid to lose me, and he knew exactly what emotional button to press: the promise of stability. For a second I lost my rational thinking, I bought a crazy wedding dress. It still hangs in my wardrobe, and the funniest thing is that it is about three sizes too small. The shop assistant must have squeezed me and watched until my lips started turning blue, then quickly released me to make a sale. Now somebody else will have the opportunity to wear this beautiful dress (that's if she is a size 12, not 18) and it will also raise money for the new local cancer centre. Every action in life has a purpose.

The wedding business caused chaos. Chris was floundering in my insecurities and my subconscious need to be a family unit again – something I have wanted since my dad was sectioned under the mental health act into a psychiatric hospital at the age of thirty-nine. (Dad never came home again.)

We had screaming, crying, and that was mainly at myself. Old scars that had healed and been covered with love-tight plasters had opened again. He wanted the best of both worlds – not to be alone and to be loved, but still creeping back to grieve for his wife. He was not ready. We had so many emotions to come to terms with to make this work, but most of all we had to consider the feelings of his children. They were still so sad, and it was too early to expect them to move out of their sadness just yet.

And then, what about me?

I don't know the answers. I am still living on gut instincts on this one, and hoping to be guided in the right direction. After all these recent painful years the direction has to be right for me.

My counselling had helped me finally establish my self-worth. It had taken forty-nine years, and I had had six months of cognitive behaviour therapy. I was not about to lose that grasp of hope for myself ever again.

Why Adrian? Why?

Helen and I were trying to make sense out of Adrian's senseless action, Helen asking questions and me avoiding the answers. It suited me at this time. My grief position was that of an emotional phobic with a heart as hard and cold as ice.

On 20 March I returned to Forest Side Hotel, Grasmere, which I had previously visited with the salsa crowd. This time I took my best friend, Janine, with me. I needed to escape and realise how lucky I was to be there in the beautiful Lake District. Grasmere, my favourite place in the Lakes, always reminds me of Wordsworth and his poem 'The Daffodils'.

Sunny days and happy memories.

When last I was at the Forest Side Hotel I wrote the very first draft of *Single Salsa Survivor*, the story of how I survived breast cancer.

Adrian has put me under immense pressure to stay alive. I will not put my mum through the grief of losing two children in her lifetime. Ironically that's not difficult for me. I have this zest for life, and I ain't giving in no matter what. I am testing my emotional status – ha ha! It is very nicely static.

What a lovely weekend Janine, my best friend, and I had in the Lake District! It gave me the space to let answers come with ease. I was still raw and scarred from the Christmas 2008 escapade, but I made up my mind to continue seeing Chris. My instincts told me to give us a chance and so did my friends. My friends wanted me to grab the chance of happiness.

I came back home to a grief capsule. Mum's face showed the deep-sealed protection of her son's name. Her face told the world she has lost a part of her heart and soul and she will never get over it. No one can imagine what it must be like. Nothing can compare with losing a child.

In the last few months Adrian had displayed some out-of-character behaviour, and we were told that he didn't want to end up living the life his dad had lived under the shadow of schizophrenia. He had been hearing voices, apparently.

Mental health has haunted our family since I was eleven, Helen was three and Adrian just one year old. Adrian was a lovely fun-loving child and I was so close to him because I looked after him and Helen throughout school holidays whilst Mum went to work. My childhood made me into the adult I am today. It gave me a benchmark for poverty, and it taught me that if I wanted anything in life I had to get it myself. Mum gave me the confidence to try anything, to never give up, and not to whinge about trivia. She gave me strong family values and the ability to love freely and show emotion. I saw her smile and enjoy Christmas on a shoestring, and she made us smile too. We didn't need lots of material things; we just needed the four of us singing at the top of our voices every time we went in the car. However short or long the journey, we sang and we sang.

What she couldn't give us was the male perspective, and that meant Adrian floundered as he grew into an adult. I think he didn't know what he was supposed to do in a relationship. I thought I had to do everything, and that's why I have two failed marriages behind me. It has taken me half a century to bury old fairytale myths and face up to my at times eccentric persona.

That eccentricity is thanks to my dad. None of us have ever given up on him. He is part of us. You wouldn't give up on somebody who had lost a limb, so why give up on mental health?

Mum taught me never to give up on my family, including my children. Many a time we criticised her when she bailed Adrian out – and, in fairness, we were probably right in the normal scheme of things – but thank God she took no notice and followed her heart.

Mum could not have done any more for Adrian than she did. I am proud of her loyalty.

Loss, Loss, Loss

My counselling sessions were helping me with my grief. Adrian's death briefly interrupted my process of recovery from the trauma of breast cancer. I had learnt to accept my own mortality, accepting that I still had challenges ahead with limited stamina, and I also now had parental responsibility for my two-year-old granddaughter, but that is another story.

Life had changed dramatically. I was adjusting to major life changes, including the loss of my career, my income and my freedom. On Christmas Day I had lost trust, self-respect and dignity, and now I had suffered the loss of my own brother. I think I was saturated in loss.

But I kept going and kept going. I was not giving up. I had faith that there would be good times once again.

The pink orchid, a flower of refinement and charm – through hard times and life's lows, the flower of dignity.

On 24 March I went out with Chris and appreciated his kindness, but I still held back on the emotion. He actually told me later that I was like a cold fish. How rude!

Chris was great company, but I was holding back. I hadn't the strength to be hurt, so I was withdrawn. As the books say, this can actually work to increase a man's interest. Chris was even more interested now I was a 'cold fish'.

Nothing in the love-ology game made sense to me and my libido was nil. How long could we put this off? Luckily he was dreading the act too, as it was the first time he had had intimacy since his wife died. It must have been such a big step for him. We had enormous problems, both of us, but it also caused us great hilarity in the bedroom, which to us is more important anyway. I scattered the bed with plastic hearts, and they kept cropping up for months afterwards. I tried to make a sensual atmosphere, but what I wanted most was a chance to be held and have that physical contact – a big hug. Chris was getting concerned about his manhood and decided to try a helping hand in the form of the famous Viagra – on prescription, of course. Oh, dearie me, what a catastrophe!

I kept saying, "Have you taken something?" as we were having tea the next day and poor Chris's bodily function was confused and remained ready for action for hour after hour. I told him not to bother again, and we have laughed ever since.

The tools are all there, but the machinery that powers the tools is a little worn and slow to start. It was not sufficiently oiled yet by freedom of mind to move on to the sexual side of the relationship, but we didn't care. Being together was enough for both of us at the moment.

Mad as it may seem, Chris and I booked a holiday to Gran Canaria, flying out on 27 April 2009. It's called 'living for the moment'. Sometimes the head can rule the heart; sometimes the heart can rule the head. In my grief I was led totally by instinct. That is how I came to enter into this relationship. Chris and I were lost souls at this time. We were not searching for the ultimate romance or the perfect lover. Both of us were fragile emotionally, and that was our bond.

The holiday was what we both needed. I had no money, but I was going as Chris's companion. I knew I needed a break, and there was a shield permanently suspended in front of my heart to protect me from loss, grief and rejection. I wanted to feel emotional pain, but it would not surface, and emotional pain from anyone else was prevented from touching any part of my soul.

Gran Canaria, 27 April to 4 May 2009

I wrote the following on a sick bag on the aeroplane. It's called writing with spontaneity.

> Once upon a time – well, eight weeks ago to be exact – the two of us were two very small fish in a very deep sea, sitting comfortably in our own homes having safe virtual liaison at the press of a computer button. Now Chris is getting to know

> the real me in such a short space of time. I have just spilt milk all over the place, scrambled egg down my top, choked on an aspirin, laughing at my own jokes. It's twenty-five minutes to landing. Chris glances over at me with affection and anticipation. I have two pieces of tissue stuck in my ears – it's to stop my ears hurting on landing.

So far so good! We had talked almost non-stop from departure lounge to landing in Gran Canaria.

The next day, 28 April, was a red-hot day. We spent our day sunbathing on what I call Amadeus Beach. The rugged volcanic scenery is the backdrop to a golden sandy beach. There is something enchanting and dramatic about Puerto Rico, and for both of us this visit to another planet was what we both needed so badly.

We had no phones, no watches – just time for us. We talked about snippets of our past, releasing something about ourselves, but we were both taking care to protect our damaged souls. We avoided those stories that could cause either of us a tear or break in our hearts. Chris had a picture of his wife in his wallet. I look a bit like her. I think he is hoping to find her, but that will never happen. There is so much pain in his eyes.

The Scruffy Jeans

We had fun moments and moments when I thought, "No, this is not for me."

Chris had quiet, reflective times and I saw the sadness shade over his eyes. He was nowhere near through the other end of his own grief. I saw it clearly.

It was the 'night of the scruffy jeans' that brought out the truth about us and any possibility of our having a future together. Chris showed me a picture of his wife, and he said he thought I was similar to her in some ways. He said he liked that resemblance and similarity, but I didn't want to be a replacement. He had lost a lot of weight, and I had hinted lots of times previous to the holiday about getting some new jeans, but he seemed trapped in the memories of the scruffy jeans. I don't know whether I was making a statement or having a mad moment, or whether it was actually the right thing to do, but I threw his old scruffy jeans right out of the complex.

Chris was gobsmacked – he couldn't believe I had done it – but I had no regrets whatsoever. I opened up and voiced my concerns about how I felt dating the complicated widower. I couldn't understand why he wanted to persevere in such a close relationship when he was so not over the loss of his wife. I told him that it wasn't the fact that he was scruffy; it was that he couldn't be bothered with himself or for me. It wasn't the first or last time I would feel utterly guilty for feeling second best; but I knew that if I was to carry on this relationship, for now that is where I would stay.

Chris didn't want us to finish our relationship. We agreed that we were both functioning at only fifty per cent love and affection level. My heart was still a block of ice from my previous let-down and from the death of my brother. Chris's wife had died of breast cancer; they had been soulmates for twenty-seven years. I had no chance of ever competing with that intense loyal time they shared. I knew that, but I wondered where I could fit in. I was under no great illusion, but the lack of intensity suited me fine for now. I wasn't ready myself. I had my own issues and my own self-preservation to think about. I had been hurt in the past and I was very cynical – not about the man, but about my own state of mind.

So much emotion behind a pair of scruffy jeans! I saw grief in its truest form, lack of motivation, can't be bothered, couldn't care less . . . I was prepared to push Chris out of his comfort zone; but, once he started to smile and enjoy life, I knew the guilt would set in. These were tense times, but we both rode the storm, both with that little bit of strength to consider our future together and a past that could never be changed.

My dysfunctional past was exposed, but there was something that kept us in unison. Was it that some power on the other side wanted us both to be happy for the remaining time we had left on this earth? Both of us deserved that.

Was I actually going to experience love that didn't hurt?

I do not underestimate the loss of a partner in death, but now I see how intense grief can follow loss of a relationship whatever its form. I have known men and women who cannot move on for many years if that flame is still flickering. In a way acceptance of loss may take longer when the loved one is still in this world. For that reason love is worth hanging on to. I know of three people who have taken their own life because of the loss of a loved one. They have all demonstrated the same behaviour to the outside world: acting out complete normality whilst carefully planning their own demise. They are clever enough to know that one slip of the tongue or one slip of emotional pain on their face will give the game away and they may be saved. Helpless are the people left behind, questioning their ability to read the signs.

For Chris and me the journey had just begun. With clearer eyes and clearer minds, and a suntan to go with it, we carried on happily for now in our special intuitive relationship. Chris is on his own journey too, and sometimes I have to get off the bus and Chris has to travel a few miles on his own. I wave and say, "That's OK. I will meet you at the next stop to continue the journey of life."

He takes the wedding ring from around his neck and places it on his little finger. He has a tattoo on his arm; his wife is with him for ever. All I had to do was fight human nature and try to be a bit more mature about the situation, but it was not easy.

I was constantly ashamed of myself for being pathetic. I felt second best and I didn't like it. But I see how lucky I am to have found this genuine person who loves so deeply. I had no choice but to allow a passage of time.

13 May 2009

What a strange day! I am really exhausted with wondering what grief is. I have felt days like this since having cancer diagnosed in 2005 – now in remission. They are what I class as 'normal reaction' days. My heart is heavy today. Mum and I keep swapping ghost stories about feeling Adrian's presence around, with phones ringing. The name Bailey keeps cropping up everywhere. We have dreams of him. Mum and I talk to him and tell him off. We want to believe he is here. We are not letting go, are we?

To Mum: There is nothing I can say to ease your pain. I wouldn't want to. There is something private about pain, and some pain is necessary to indicate to a person they can still feel emotion. There is nothing comparable to the loss of a child. I can't even imagine it without panic setting in.

June 2009

We can't lay flowers. There is no grave where the ashes are scattered, but we let off balloons into the sky and watched them rise and fly into the distance until they disappeared.

Happy fortieth birthday, Adrian xxxxxxxxxx.

The Memorial Gig, 8 June 2009

So, so many friends in one room, such an appreciation of Adrian's life, but he died alone!

We are a musical family – even my son has started singing lessons. He is heading for *The X Factor*. Lisa, my other daughter, continues to dance, and Erica, Fiona's daughter, continues to grow and make us all laugh. Fiona wrote and sang a song for Adrian at the Memorial Gig. She is amazingly talented, and the song has so much meaning.

If only . . .

The suicide jigsaw is slowly coming together, but only Adrian knows the final piece. We know he had lost his soulmate and he felt betrayal and rejection. A broken heart, fear, despair and poverty were the ingredients for suicide. If only he had added time and friends and family to life's mixture, he might have still been alive today.

If only Adrian could have known that time heals! Sometimes the hardest thing to do is wait. Sometimes the hardest thing in life is to reach out for help.

In the room that night of the Memorial Gig I saw how his life was so musically orientated – a creative, chaotic world.

If only I had been more forthcoming in seeing him and appreciating his lifestyle rather than thinking that being a musician is not a proper job! The irony is that all my children have an artistic leaning and I understand their vocation.

Fiona has been particularly affected by the loss because Adrian had an affinity with Fiona that she I am sure didn't have with anybody else.

IF ONLY

Why didn't he call me and say,
"Help me. Help me, I plan to die.
Just for one moment, why didn't you try to
Think of me,
Think of Mum,
Think of Dad,
Think of Helen.
We all would have run to you,
Picked you up and carried you for a while,
Until you felt strong enough to walk the path of life again,
To face the world and smile.

If only! You're like a star and we miss you.

Baby Clinic, 11 September 2009

I used to work at the baby clinic not that long ago, and there are items all around the room that I have placed there. They are still there in good working order, never needing to be replaced. It represents a period in my life when I plodded in normality, when tragedies and illness and divorce happened to other people and it was my job to support them. There is a broccoli balloon hanging from the ceiling. It's been there since 2006 and it's still inflated. And the old kitchen clock, donated by me, works perfectly. It shows that if something works, then leave it alone. Happy memories come back to me of work with my colleagues, great comradeship, worrying about trivia and consoling each other after petty arguments with partners and after the kids have played us up yet again. Thriving to achieve in our careers, dedicated to work, we were all trained nurses, but for two of us life was about to change dramatically.

Now Catherine, my dear friend, is sitting on the floor with me and Erica, my granddaughter. I ask how she is.

Her life has changed dramatically too. Catherine has been catapulted harshly to Cancer Planet, as her daughter, Lucy, has had to endure months of intensive treatment for leukaemia. Then from Cancer Planet she had to fly briefly to Grief City as her dad died recently of breast cancer.

I ask her how she feels.
"I don't know," she replies.
All the hurt and sadness lies deep within her eyes.
"I am on another planet" were her very own words.
I said, "I know that planet."
Transport is by grief capsule only –
A passport identified by loss.
Destination Grief City.

Today I shared a moment and found
What grief is about –
An inner sadness so private it cannot be shared,
About how we don't have enough tears
To express how sad we feel.
Grief comes to those who wait,
No matter how many seconds
Of the day and night we try to fill.
Grief finds us and our hearts stand still.
If you are looking for grief and cannot find tears,
Reach out your hands and release your fears.

Thank goodness both of us in the past didn't have a crystal ball.

Love life,
Live life,
Friends for life.

Thanks to Cancer Research, Lucy is well now and has finished her treatment.

2 September 2009

Seven whole months – twenty-eight weeks or 196 days – have passed and still no cry! My reaction is one of disbelief, trance-like behaviour, especially when I hear a Beatles song on the radio or a band is playing in the distance.

The Inquest

The inquest was surreal. I remember thinking how traditional the courtroom was, and we all sat with linked arms. There was only Chris, me, Helen, Mum and Mike, my stepdad, sitting in the front row. A young man in a police uniform was there to give a statement about the night's events on 5 March 2009, when he broke down the barricaded door and found a male in his thirties hanging from a homemade gallows. There was a note screwed up and thrown into a corner as if he was angry. His decision made, Adrian did the deed. What affected me most was that the judge stated Adrian had only a small amount of alcohol in his bloodstream. I was devastated. I wanted him to have been out-of-his-head drunk so that he would not have felt anything and so that I would know he couldn't possibly have been in control of his actions.

Two weeks before the dreaded deed he came to see me and I asked him to stay with me. He said he was busy and had things to do. I never thought he was planning to just up and leave me.

The Complicated Widower, 14 September 2009

My cancer journey, as I have said before, was my own journey – nobody else's, only mine. I was in complete control, single and had no partner to consider.

Now I have a bereaved partner and his children and we are on the bus again. It's a pity it is not a comfortable coach with a tour guide helping us to make the right decisions in order for us to be a non-complicated couple.

I knew that dates were going to be a problem – birthdays, wedding anniversaries, Christmas. Why don't we just say 365 days of the year? I wonder if any one day passes by when his wife doesn't flash through his mind. I think I am coping a little better lately with my hot-and-cold lover. In fact, the more he makes me feel secure in our relationship, the easier I am finding his grief relapses.

It's not so easy when it comes to his youngest daughter. At times I really want to give her a hug; then I want to shout at her. She deliberately tries to sabotage our relationship at times. I suppose I understand her feeling like that, but I hate being the other woman – hate it! Both of us, Chris and I, wonder at the easy way out – but no, we fight on because our love is worth it.

Sometimes silence is welcomed; sometimes I wish it would cease – but silence is my inspiration to write.

I am off on another holiday with Chris again. We are still together, but the path of romance has not been easy. Being the partner of a widower sometimes makes me feel as though I am in some torrid love affair. Chris gives his body – well, even that's an issue. Widowers sometimes can't give you much at all, but Chris is trying so hard to please me. He is trying to fix my garden, my house, my problems, but he can't yet fix my heart or my insecurities about my position in his life. I have to admire this man for trying. He is a good person, a kind person and full of fun. He makes me laugh, and that is my recipe for the number one in my life, so we carry on. What I have to tell myself sometimes is, "Don't fall into the trap of being grateful for his affection, and don't accept less than I want out of the relationship." I cannot settle for less. I have learnt to live by myself, but most of all to love myself. I am changed. I now have self-worth. In previous relationships I made the mistake of feeling forever in their debt for some reason or another, such as having young children, having a disfigurement after breast surgery or having a dysfunctional family history. In my second marriage the only debt was the debt found on a credit card.

Now I am in a loving relationship with a widower. We play at happy families and homemaking. I have rings of commitment and trust.

This is a hard time for Chris and his family, and it is clearly going to take time for me to be accepted by his daughters. Can you blame them? I don't, and so I try hard to consider their needs as well as my own and ignore the games that are sometimes played to get their dad back to honour the time with their mum. I understand.

A similar scenario occurred for me when I first attended a meeting as a manager in the NHS. What could I say? Words are all very well, but actions speak louder than words. I could promise them the world and say what a wonderful person I was, but I knew they would be wary. Instead I told them I could only promise to support them as a manager, involve them with decisions and be honest with them. Time would show how we got along as a team. Respect is earnt – it is never free. I was prepared to apologise and take responsibility if things didn't go to plan, but on the other hand I wanted to give my team the stability of knowing my convictions were supported by good reasoning. The most important thing of all was that we all had the same aim to care to the highest standard for our patients.

This fits in very nicely with my present situation as the widower's girlfriend. I can't expect his daughters to believe that I care for them and understand their loss; I can't expect them to like me, but I hope they will in time. I am not even going to try to replace their mum. What an absurd thought! I am not going to bring my views into their house or change things. What matters most is that we all love their dad and have the same aim – his happiness.

Sometimes things don't quite work out as we hope because none of us is perfect. I have good intentions, but human nature kicks in. I have so much inbred insecurity that I sometimes can't follow the widower's girlfriend's handbook of the ideal. Then I run away. I want to jump out of their memories because I feel guilty for living. Their mum died and I am still here.

I tell myself again and again I am worthy of my existence.

The family home is an issue. Memories of his wife are everywhere in the house – where she sat on the sofa and family photos. I feel haunted by her presence – an impostor. I tried helping out and cleaning, but that was a big mistake as I touched and moved personal items. I was wrong to do this and I learnt from it, although I had good intentions. I was insensitive and I upset Chris's youngest daughter.

The house is for sale and that is good. The family need to hold their memories of happy times, and the longer they stay in this house without his wife the more grief is taking its toll on all of them. The youngest daughter was stuck in her grief and clung to the family home, the safety net of the four walls. It was all she had left of her mum and memories of times as a family, her dreams shattered and her ally gone for ever. I feel for her, but I am not the one to help her. She is isolated in a village with only her mum's grave as company.

Chris was accessing support from Cruse. There are no relatives nearby – only her sister and dad, who were grieving themselves, and of course *me*! Her whole life was affected, and this also affected Chris. He couldn't make things better for his child, and as a parent this is the hardest pill ever to swallow.

Chris was never going to sell his home. As he took prospective buyers around he sadly told them of the loss of his wife and how the house was his 'empire'.

I said, "Do you want to move on or stay in memories? Your home is becoming a dungeon rather than a castle."

This is how Daisy Lane should be presented to the prospective buyer:

Daisy Lane

The house of sunshine where everywhere you turn and everywhere you walk the sun hits your face and warms your heart.

Ambiance of tranquillity and an air of luxury – an honour to stay at Daisy Lane.

There is no uniformity about Daisy Lane. Can't you see that is its charm? You will not change Daisy Lane; so do not venture if you cannot appreciate the uniqueness of its character and personality.

Sadness is present. It has been a home and castle for many years, happiness of family life resounding in every room, but now it's time for the family to leave – no regrets, only serenity. The past is left behind.

If you are brave enough to venture into the secret garden, close your eyes and dream. There are no boundaries in the Daisy Lane garden. Every flower, every shrub has its place and their natural beauty is intertwined with the personality of the garden's owners.

To live at Daisy Lane is to love Daisy Lane. Nothing less will do. If you feel in every way the beauty I describe – if you do – Daisy Lane the family will give to you.

Laughter whistles through the trees;
Colours rage, an effervescent show.
In each bloom and plant that grows
Happy times of family life
We know.

This beauty is not for me and Chris. We have to move on. We have to move away and start afresh – a new life, new house, new memories – new family photos. But I hope Chris brings with him his old values. He loved and cared deeply for his wife; I want to feel that love too for me alone as his partner.

Zante

We flew off on another holiday. We were running away, I think because, with external pressures from both sides, we couldn't get to grips with how we felt about one another. To escape was the only way. These breaks tested our relationship, and Zante, in Greece, was certainly the place we were tested the most. Chris had some very strange times during this holiday, and it was make or break. There will be no winners in this game of love, but I felt that if things didn't get better I might be tempted to throw in the towel.

'Should I give up, or should I just keep chasing pavements' even if I lose my way?

Zante – mesmerising, romantic Zante!

Five months after our holiday in Gran Canaria how life had changed! What I am going to write is absurd, but it reflects my personality: I believe in fairy tales. I know fairy tales come true. You just have to believe, take risks and have faith that any outcome is meant to be.

My children have achieved dreams just by believing in fairy tales and themselves. Whether this is right or wrong, none of us have regrets.

To follow a dream wear new shoes.
To catch a dream shoes must be worn.

Let's just reminisce about how dreams can come true.

Lisa was in the Royal Ballet from the age of seven and she has performed and toured with Birmingham Royal Ballet. I have often waited at the stage door for her to come out after a performance. She had the talent, but children need their parents' support both financially and morally, and their parents need to give their time. If, like me, you haven't got money, you find ways and means. I wanted her to have a chance to achieve her dreams and to spend her working life doing what she loves best – dancing. Lisa spent three years at dance school and she loved it. She worked hard every day, dancing and improving her technique. How proud I was and what pleasure I got from seeing her dance!

Alistair had amazing football skills. How I loved the day we went to trials for Manchester City! I wore a badge he had made me at school, and I just panicked because if he was chosen I had no idea how I would take him to Manchester to train. If you think too much about doing something, you will never do it. As Lisa would say, "Just go, girl!"

When Ali flew off to Magaluf to work in the sun, I said, "Go, enjoy, have fun, gain confidence." Dare I mention that I went over twice to make sure he was safe and OK! It was the best thing he ever did. He escaped my sadness and the depression in the household, caused by the nasty taste of illness and fear of losing a loved one.

Then there is Fiona. Fiona just does anything she wants to, and I wouldn't swap her for the world. We stand in queues for *Britain's Got Talent*. She is a socialite, which intrigues me, and a model. What can I say! She achieved her dream at four months' pregnant and made the front cover of – thank goodness! – a reputable magazine.

Life may be chaotic and unpredictable, but it's never boring.

Back to Zante. Zante has horse-drawn carriages, quaint churches, sunshine, sea, sand, bars on the beach, palm trees and crimson flowers. My fairy tale ran away with me and I got into big trouble this time. I jeopardised my relationship, but I couldn't see why Chris couldn't join in my impulsive behaviour. Why couldn't he just indulge me in my wishes for one day?

I planned a 'commitment day' for us, and we rode our bikes to the church. I dressed my bike and my hair in crimson flowers, and I wore a pretty white skirt and top. My only thought was 'Hey, look how much money we are saving, going through the motions for the price of a cup of coffee in the Palm Café on the beach.' I thought it was romantic, but Chris thought differently – and he was to tell me so in no uncertain terms.

I am dreamer. I write poems; I write stories. I cry at Disney films. That's me, and it gets me into trouble. What I love most of all is a good love story, but Chris makes sure I step back into reality. He told me straight. He was ready fully for me to be his partner but no way his wife.

We had a debate and I felt embarrassed and silly, and of course hurt. I am ready, after being single now for so many years, to settle down. I like being that extra-special person to somebody. I crave traditional family life and to be again the wife of somebody who cares for me. It is the dream of getting married.

I'm your partner, not your wife,
I'm your companion, not your mate,
I'm your— Well, what am I?

Those moments of grief I see in your face
Cut through my heart like a knife.
You feel guilty;
I feel guilty.

He loves me,
He loves me not.
Maybe – maybe not.

Christmas Eve, 2009

Another precious year has passed and I think I remember every one of the 364 days since last Christmas. I didn't know a year ago that within twenty-four hours my life plan was to change yet again, that I would be a shell-shocked casualty of life's unpredictability, questioning why it kept happening to me and wondering what was in store for me next. Little did I know that I would be catapulted into grief and happiness. Now, on Christmas Eve 2009, I am here and my brother isn't and Chris's wife isn't, but we are. I believe, from the things that have happened this year – the good things – that our guardian angels are with us at all times. They help us when, as Chris puts it, curved balls are thrown at us.

My loss lives on. I remember his blonde curls and his tiny fingers under the door when he should have been in bed. I remember times when we had play fights, and he always won because I would be laughing so much. My heart wrenches, and inside I yearn to hear him sing: "Let it be, let it be, let it be, let it be. Speaking words of wisdom, let it be."

22 January 2010

Christmas and New Year went without a hitch. I was totally chilled and happy. I spent a romantic few days in the Lakes in my favourite place, Grasmere. This time snow lay on the ground – a magical setting. The Forest Side Hotel had changed. It's funny how bricks and mortar change and become a memory, as do people. It's impossible to recreate happy memories – that's why we have to move on and make new beginnings.

I'm still making mistakes, living with grief. Chris and the girls have moved house and I helped them. I thought I should be there to support them, but maybe that was a mistake. It was time for the three of them to say goodbye. All their lifetime memories were in boxes – some of those boxes to be kept closed now. I left and went home.

I always thought I had the maturity to handle anything in the right way, but this living with grief thing has floored me on numerous occasions. It has been necessary for both of us to have the same commitment to carry on and not take the easy way out and give up.

Chris's eldest daughter has always been accepting of her dad's need to love again; the youngest daughter has had reservations, but we have slowly worked out where our bond starts and finishes. After Christmas we tested the boundaries and, although I was devastated and felt I had failed, that was my problem.

I asked myself the question, "How do you feel, Sharon, living with grief?"

I feel sorry that Chris has lost his wife, and sorry that the girls have lost their mum. I can't bring her back and I never knew her. I can only try to show sympathy.

How do I feel?

Guilty and ashamed at my resentment of someone who has died, angry at myself, ignorant about how to respond to families in grief, I still feel second best.

I tried to step into Chris's wife's shoes and walk the same path, but the shoes do not fit and I tripped over and fell. It's time to wear my own shoes, walk a different path with different soles and different steps along the way. Remember when I used to get of the bus and let Chris journey on his own? Well, the bus route changed. They reached their final destination together the day she died. Chris had no choice but to wave goodbye.

It's time for Chris and me to stay on the bus together now and follow a new route to an unknown destination.

We have no clue where we are going, but we are both in the front seat, him driving sometimes and me others; him navigating sometimes and me others.

I feel so sorry for the girls, and I have built in time a genuine affection for both of them. I will be there for them when they need me. They are a part of Chris, and therefore they are important to me. I am sorry they have lost the one and only person who understood them, forgave them and loved them unconditionally. I am so sorry, girls.

For Adrian

Now 25 February is looming. It will be a year since that day you arranged your exit from the world. I am retracing your steps to picture you in your kitchen looking for food – but no, we are not in a country where we will starve. I picture you isolated in your flat – but no, we must get out. Walk, walk till we see so many human beings in one day we are glad to get home to peace and tranquillity. The disease of silence is temporary; it will not kill us. I have felt despair, humiliation and poverty, but every time I relied on the fact that I knew there would be a good tomorrow or the next day. Bad, good, bad, good, bad, good – that is life. I wish I could have just said to you, "Keep fighting. Life is precious, and there are so many here who love you."

I am sorry I didn't help you. I am sorry I didn't save you.

For Chris

Two years have passed since the death of your wife. You have left my side and stepped on the bus again – the one that takes you on a journey of grief. I saw you looking out of the window, searching for your past again. I am calling you to get off the bus and meet me at the next stop. Can you hear me? I'm here. Look around and you will see *me.*

When you shed a tear
I am always here
For you.

For Me, 28 February 2010, My Fiftieth Birthday

I am not really in the mood to celebrate my birthday and I am angry at Adrian for taking my special day away from me. I worked so damn hard to reach my birthday four years ago, after I had my second chemotherapy. But oh, I was so grateful to be celebrating my life that day with friends! Sharon, keep hold of that memory.

Chris is not in the mood, either, to celebrate my birthday. He is antagonistic towards me, and I am angry at him for making me feel not worthy of my existence. We have had a really rough week emotionally, and I have thrown my rings away. Perhaps I'm being totally irresponsible, but I was gutted when he said he was not ready to commit. I know that I have such a pathetic side to me – so many insecurities plus human nature. And spitting out the dummy too! I do love the stability and permanency of being married.

I remember how lonely I felt when I had no one to moan about, and now Chris is making me breakfast and he has surprised me with a trip to Dublin. He is trying his best through thick and thin, and you, Sharon, need to appreciate this wonderful man for his good qualities and stop feeling sorry for yourself, girl.

Sometimes we do not know the reason why, but I know today, my fiftieth birthday, was the day I broke down and cried. Before I still shed tears, but they were disguised in the written word; and now I wipe my eyes.

Gran Canaria, 27 April to 4 May 2010

A year on and we are here together in the same place, but we are two people who have grown in character and who have learnt again many of life's lessons. The strain and grief has left Chris's face, and his wife is safe in a place within his heart. The twenty-seven years of love and marriage are a wonderful memory, but Chris is now moving on and joining me on my path of life.

As we walk together in the sand looking out to sea we are both staring in the same direction – at our future as future husband and wife. We have no idea of what lies ahead, but we do not need to know because at no time will we travel life separately again. On 8 October 2010 we get married. For our honeymoon we have booked to go again to our special island of love – Gran Canaria. We are travelling on 29 November – five years to the day since I was diagnosed with breast cancer. A honeymoon and a celebration – yes, a celebration of life!

So with that I say, “Love life, live life.” This is the start of another chapter of my life.

Glide into your future with poise and ease,
Memories stored in every tear.
Don't look behind you –
The past has gone.
Love is with you.
It's time to move on.

To my mum and all those who,
like us, have lost a loved one.

A leg of ham was on
a tray.
Kevin took the ham
away.

Then he hid it from his dad.

Kevin had been very bad.

‘Look,’ said Dad. ‘The ham has gone.

Is this something you have done?’

Kevin was red.

Kevin was sad.

'Yes. I hid it,' he said to Dad.

So Kevin went to get the ham.

'I am sorry. I really am.'

'You and Lotty eat it up.

I have been a silly pup.'